ELECTION

A SERMON

I0159848

DELIVERED BY
THE REV.
C. H. SPURGEON

a lamp post book

ELECTION: A SERMON

By C.H.Spurgeon

The Sermons of Rev. Spurgeon are in the Public Domain.

Format and Layout Copyright © 2008 by LAMP PoST Inc.

Copyright © 2008 by LAMP PoST Inc. All rights reserved.

Print ISBN 10: 1-60039-100-1

Print ISBN 13: 978-1-60039-100-2

ebook ISBN 10: 1-60039-703-4

ebook ISBN 13: 978-1-60039-703-5

Published by Lamp Post Inc.

www.lamppostpubs.com

For whom he did foreknow, he also did predestinate [to be] conformed to the image of his Son, that he might be the firstborn among many brethren. Moreover whom he did predestinate, them he also called: and whom he called, them he also justified: and whom he justified, them he also glorified. What shall we then say to these things? If God [be] for us, who [can be] against us? He that spared not his own Son, but delivered him up for us all, how shall he not with him also freely give us all things? Who shall lay any thing to the charge of God's elect?

ROMANS 8:29-33

THE REV. C. H. SPURGEON.
ELLIOTT & FRY,   Copyright.   55, BAKER ST.

THE REV.

CHARLES HADDON SPURGEON

The descendant of several generations of Independent ministers, he was born at Kelvedon, Essex, and became a Baptist in 1850. In the same year he preached his first sermon, and in 1852 he was appointed paster of the Baptist congregation at Waterbeach. In 1854 he went to Southwark, where his sermons drew such crowds that a new church, the Metropolitan Tabernacle in Newington Causeway, had to be built for him. Apart from his preaching activites he founded a pastors' college, an orphanage, and a colportage association for the propagation of uplifting literature. Spurgeon was a strong Calvinist. He had a controversy in 1864 with the Evangelical party of the Church of England for remaining in a Church that taught Baptismal Regeneration, and also estranged considerable sections of his own community by rigid opposition to the more liberal methods of Biblical exegesis. These differences led to a rupture with the Baptist Union in 1887. He owed his fame as a preacher to his great oratorical gifts, humour, and shrewd common sense, which showed itself especially in his treatment of contemporary problems. Among his works are The Saint and his Saviour (1857), Commenting and Commentaries (1876) and numerous volumes of sermons (translated into many languages).

—*The Oxford Dictionary of the Christian Church*

ELECTION

A SERMON
(NO. 41-42)

DELIVERED ON SABBATH MORNING,
SEPTEMBER 2, 1855
BY THE REV. C. H. SPURGEON
AT NEW PARK STREET CHAPEL, SOUTHWARK.

"But we are bound to give thanks always to God for you, brethren beloved of the Lord, because God hath from the beginning chosen you to salvation through sanctification of the Spirit and belief of the truth: Whereunto he called you by our gospel, to the obtaining of the glory of our Lord Jesus Christ." — 2 Thessalonians 2:13-14.

IF there were no other text in the sacred Word except this one, I think we should all be bound to receive and acknowledge the truthfulness of the great and glorious doctrine of God's ancient choice of his family. But there seems to be an inveterate prejudice in the human mind against this doctrine; and although most other doctrines will be received by professing Christians, some with caution, others with pleasure, yet this one seems to be most frequently disregarded and discarded. In many of our pulpits it would be reckoned a high sin and treason to preach a sermon upon election, because they could not make it what they call a "practical" discourse. I believe they have erred from the truth therein. Whatever God has revealed, he has revealed for a purpose. There is nothing in Scripture which may not, under the influence of God's Spirit, be turned into a practical discourse: for "all Scripture is given by inspiration of God, and is profitable" for some purpose of spiritual usefulness. It is true, it may not be turned into a free-will discourse—that we know right well—but it can be turned into a practical free-grace discourse: and free-grace practice is the best practice, when the true doctrines of God's immutable love are brought to bear upon the hearts of saints and sinners. Now, I trust this morning some of you who are startled at the very sound of this word, will say, "I will give it a fair hearing; I will lay aside my prejudices; I will just hear what this man has to say." Do not shut your ears and say at once, "It is high doctrine." Who has authorized you to call it high or low? Why should you oppose yourself to God's doctrine? Remember what became of the children who found fault with God's prophet, and exclaimed, "Go up, thou bald-head; go up, thou bald-head." Say nothing against God's doctrines, lest haply some evil beast should come out of the forest and devour you also. There are other woes beside the open judgment of heaven— take heed that these fall not on your head. Lay aside your prejudices: listen calmly, listen dispassionately: hear what Scripture says; and when you receive the truth, if God should be pleased to reveal and manifest it to your souls, do not be ashamed to confess it. To confess you were wrong yesterday, is only to acknowledge that you are a little wiser to-day; and instead of being a reflection on yourself, it is an honour to your judgment, and shows that you are improving in the knowledge of the truth. Do not be ashamed to learn, and to cast aside your old doctrines and views, but to take up that which you may more plainly see to be in the Word of God. But if you do not see it to be here in the Bible, whatever I may say, or whatever authorities I may plead, I beseech you, as you love your souls, reject it; and if from this pulpit you ever hear things contrary to this Sacred Word, remember that the Bible must be the first, and God's minister must lie underneath it. We must not stand on the Bible to preach, but we must preach with the Bible above our heads. After all we have preached, we are well aware that the mountain of truth is higher than our eyes can discern; clouds and darkness are round about its summit, and we cannot discern its topmost pinnacle; yet we will try to preach it as well as we can. But since we are mortal, and liable to err, exercise your judgment; "Try the spirits whether they are of God"; and if on mature reflection on your bended knees, you are led to disregard election—a thing which I consider to be utterly impossible—then forsake it; do not hear it preached, but believe and confess whatever you see to be God's Word. I can say no more than that by way of exordium.

Now, first, I shall speak a little concerning the truthfulness of this doctrine: "God hath from the beginning chosen you to salvation." Secondly, I shall try to prove that this election is absolute: "He hath from the beginning chosen you to salvation," not for sanctification, but "through sanctification of the Spirit and belief of the truth." Thirdly, this election is eternal, because the text says, "God hath from the beginning chosen you." Fourthly, it is personal: "He hath chosen you." Then we will look at the effects of the doctrine—see what it does; and lastly, as God may enable us, we will try and look at its tendencies, and see whether it is indeed a terrible and licentious doctrine. We will take the flower, and like true bees, see whether there be any honey whatever in it; whether any good can come of it, or whether it is an unmixed, undiluted evil.

I. First, I must try and prove that the doctrine is TRUE. And let me begin with an argumentum ad hominem; I will speak to you according to your different positions and stations. There are some of you who belong to the Church of England, and I am happy to see so many of you here. Though now and then I certainly say some very hard things about Church and State, yet I love the old Church, for she has in her communion many godly ministers and eminent saints. Now, I know you are great believers in what the Articles declare to be sound doctrine. I will give you a specimen of what they utter concerning election, so that if you believe them, you cannot avoid receiving election. I will read a portion of the 17th Article upon Predestination and Election:—

"Predestination to life is the everlasting purpose of God, whereby (before the foundations of the world were laid) he hast continually decreed by his counsel secret to us, to deliver from curse and damnation those whom he hath chosen in Christ out of mankind, and to bring them by Christ to everlasting salvation, as vessels made to honour. Wherefore they which be endued with so excellent a benefit of God be called according to God's purpose by his Spirit working in due season: they through grace obey the calling: they be justified freely: they be made sons of God by adoption: they be made like the image of his only-begotten Son Jesus Christ: they walk religiously in good works, and at length, by God's mercy, they attain to ever-lasting felicity."

Now, I think any churchman, if he be a sincere and honest believer in Mother Church, must be a thorough believer in election. True, if he turns to certain other portions of the Prayer Book, he will find things contrary to the doctrines of free-grace, and altogether apart from scriptural teaching; but if he looks at the Articles, he must see that God hath chosen his people unto eternal life. I am not so desperately enamoured, however, of that book as you may be; and I have only used this Article to show you that if you belong to the Establishment of England you should at least offer no objection to this doctrine of predestination.

Another human authority whereby I would confirm the doctrine of election, is, the old Waldensian creed. If you read the creed of the old Waldenses, emanating from them in the midst of the burning heat of persecution, you will see that these renowned professors and confessors of the Christian faith did most firmly receive and embrace this doctrine, as being a portion of the truth of God. I have copied from an old book one of the Articles of their faith:—

"That God saves from corruption and damnation those whom he has chosen from the foundations of the world, not for any disposition, faith, or holiness that he foresaw in them, but of his mere mercy in Christ Jesus his Son, passing by all the rest according to the irreprehensible reason of his own free-will and justice."

It is no novelty, then, that I am preaching; no new doctrine. I love to proclaim these strong old doctrines, which are called by nickname Calvinism, but which are surely and verily the revealed truth of God as it is in Christ Jesus. By this truth I make a pilgrimage into the past, and as I go, I see father after father, confessor after confessor, martyr after martyr, standing up to shake hands with me. Were I a Pelagian, or a believer in the doctrine of free-will, I should have to walk for centuries all alone. Here and there a heretic of no very honourable character might rise up and call me brother. But taking these things to be the standard of my faith, I see the land of the ancients peopled with my brethren—I behold multitudes who confess the same as I do, and acknowledge that this is the religion of God's own church.

I also give you an extract from the old Baptist Confession. We are Baptists in this congregation—the greater part of us at any rate—and we like to see what our own forefathers wrote. Some two hundred years ago the Baptists assembled together, and published their articles of faith, to put an end to certain reports against their orthodoxy which had gone forth to the world. I turn to this old book—which I have just published [The Baptist Confession of Faith (1689)]— and I find the following as the 3rd Article: "By the decree of God, for the manifestation of his glory, some men and angels are predestinated, or foreordained to eternal life through Jesus Christ to the praise of his glorious grace; others being left to act in their sin to their just condemnation, to the praise of his glorious justice. These angels and men thus predestinated and foreordained, are particularly and unchangeably designed, and their number so certain and definite, that it cannot be either increased or diminished. Those of mankind that are predestinated to life, God, before the foundation of the world was laid, according to his eternal and immutable purpose, and the secret counsel and good pleasure of his will, hath chosen in Christ unto everlasting glory out of his mere free grace and love, without any other thing in the creature as a condition or cause moving him thereunto."

As for these human authorities, I care not one rush for all three of them. I care not what they say, pro or con, as to this doctrine. I have only used them as a kind of confirmation to your faith, to show you that whilst I may be railed upon as a heretic and as a hyper-Calvinist, after all I am backed up by antiquity. All the past stands by me. I do not care for the present. Give me the past and I will hope for the future. Let the present rise up in my teeth, I will not care. What though a host of the churches of London may have forsaken the great cardinal doctrines of God, it matters not. If a handful of us stand alone in an unflinching maintenance of the sovereignty of our God, if we are beset by enemies, ay, and even by our own brethren, who ought to be our friends and helpers, it matters not, if we can but count upon the past; the noble army of martyrs, the glorious host of confessors, are our friends; the witnesses of truth stand by us. With these for us, we will not say that we stand alone, but we may exclaim, "Lo, God hath reserved unto himself seven thousand that have not bowed the knee unto Baal." But the best of all is, God is with us.

The great truth is always the Bible, and the Bible alone. My hearers, you do not believe in any other book than the Bible, do you? If I could prove this from all the books in Christendom; if I could fetch back the Alexandrian library, and prove it thence, you would not believe it any more; but you surely will believe what is in God's Word.

I have selected a few texts to read to you. I love to give you a whole volley of texts when I am afraid you will distrust a truth, so that you may be too astonished to doubt, if you do not in reality believe. Just let me run through a catalogue of passages where the people of God are called elect. Of course if the people are called elect, there must be election. If Jesus Christ and his apostles were accustomed to style believers by the title of elect, we must certainly believe that they were so, otherwise the term does not mean anything.

Jesus Christ says, "Except that the Lord had shortened those days, no flesh should be saved; but for the elect's sake, whom he hath chosen, he hath shortened the days." "False Christs and false prophets shall rise, and shall shew signs and wonders, to seduce, if it were possible, even the elect." "Then shall he send his angels, and shall gather together his elect from the four winds, from the uttermost part of the earth to the uttermost part of heaven" (Mark 13:20, 22, 27). "Shall not God avenge his own elect, who cry day and night unto him, though he bear long with them?" (Luke 18:7). Together with many other passages which might be selected, wherein either the word "elect," or "chosen," or "foreordained," or "appointed" is mentioned; or the phrase "my sheep" or some similar designation, showing that Christ's people are distinguished from the rest of mankind.

But you have concordances, and I will not trouble you with texts. Throughout the epistles, the saints are constantly called "the elect." In the Colossians we find Paul saying, "Put on therefore, as the elect of God, holy and beloved, bowels of mercies." When he writes to Titus, he calls himself, "Paul, a servant of God, and an apostle of Jesus Christ, according to the faith of God's elect." Peter says, "Elect according to the foreknowledge of God the Father." Then if you turn to John, you will find he is very fond of the word. He says, "The elder to the elect lady"; and he speaks of our "elect sister." And we know where it is written, "The church that is at Babylon, elected together with you." They were not ashamed of the word in those days; they were not afraid to talk about it. Now-a-days the word has been dressed up with diversities of meaning, and persons have mutilated and marred the doctrine, so that they have made it a very doctrine of devils, I do confess; and many who call themselves believers, have gone to rank Antinomianism. But notwithstanding this, why should I be ashamed of it, if men do wrest it? We love God's truth on the rack, as well as when it is walking upright. If there were a martyr whom we loved before he came on the rack, we should love him more still when he was stretched there. When God's truth is stretched on the rack, we do not call it falsehood. We love not to see it racked, but we love it even when racked, because we can discern what its proper proportions ought to have been if it had not been racked and tortured by the cruelty and inventions of men. If you will read many of the epistles of the ancient fathers, you will find them always writing to the people of God as the "elect." Indeed the common conversational term used among many of the churches by the primitive Christians to one another was that of the "elect." They would often use the term to one another, showing that it was generally believed that all God's people were manifestly "elect."

But now for the verses that will positively prove the doctrine. Open your Bibles and turn to John 15:16, and there you will see that Jesus Christ has chosen his people, for he says, "Ye have not chosen me, but I have chosen you, and ordained you, that ye should go and bring forth fruit, and that your fruit should remain: that whatsoever ye shall ask of the Father in my name, he may give it you." Then in the 19th verse, "If ye were of the world, the world would love his own; but because ye are not of the world, but I have chosen you out of the world, therefore the world hateth you." Then in the 17th chapter and the 8th and 9th verses, "For I have given unto them the words which thou gavest me; and they have received them and have known surely that I came out from thee, and they have believed that thou didst send me. I pray for them: I pray not for the world, but for them which thou hast given me; for they are thine." Turn to Acts 13:48: "And when the Gentiles heard this, they were glad, and glorified the word of the Lord; and as many as were ordained to eternal life believed." They may try to split that passage into hairs if they like; but it says, "ordained to eternal life" in the original as plainly as it possibly can; and we do not care about all the different commentaries thereupon. You scarcely need to be reminded of Romans 8, because I trust you are all well acquainted with that chapter and understand it by this time. In the 29th and following verses, it says, "For whom he did foreknow, he also did predestinate to be conformed to the image of his Son, that he might be the first-born among many brethren. Moreover, whom he did predestinate, them he also called: and whom he called, them he also justified; and whom he justified, them he also glorified. What shall we then say to these things? If God be for us, who can be against us? He that spared not his own Son, but delivered him up for us all, how shall he not with him also freely give us all things? Who shall lay anything to the charge of God's elect?" It would also be unnecessary to repeat the whole of the 9th chapter of Romans. As long as that remains in the Bible, no man shall be able to prove Arminianism; so long as that is written there, not the most violent contortions of the passage will ever be able to exterminate the doctrine of election from the Scriptures. Let us read such verses as these — "For the children being not yet born, neither having done any good or evil, that the purpose of God according to election might stand, not of works, but of him that calleth; it was said unto her, The elder shall serve the younger." Then read the 22nd verse, "What if God, willing to show his wrath, and to make his power known, endured with much longsuffering the vessels of wrath fitted to destruction. And that he might make known the riches of his glory on the vessels of mercy, which he had afore prepared unto glory." Then go on to Romans 11:7 — "What then? Israel hath not obtained that which he seeketh for; but the election hath obtained it, and the rest were blinded." In the 5th verse of the same chapter, we read — "Even so then at this present time also there is a remnant according to the election of grace." You, no doubt, all recollect the passage in I Corinthians 1:26-29: "For ye see your calling, brethren, how that not many wise men after the flesh, not many mighty, not many noble, are called: but God hath chosen the foolish things of the world to confound the wise; and God hath chosen the weak things of the world to confound the things which are mighty; and base things of the world, and things which are despised, hath God chosen, yea, and things which are not, to bring to nought things which are: that no flesh should glory in his presence." Again, remember the passage in I Thessalonians 5:9 — "God hath not appointed us to wrath, but to obtain salvation by our Lord Jesus Christ." And then you have my text, which methinks would be quite enough. But, if you need any more, you can find them at your leisure, if we have not quite removed your suspicions as to the doctrine not being true.

Methinks, my friends, that this overwhelming mass of Scripture testimony must stagger those who dare to laugh at this doctrine. What shall we say of those who have so often despised it, and denied its divinity; who have railed at its justice, and dared to defy God and call him an Almighty tyrant, when they have heard of his having elected so many to eternal life? Canst thou, O rejector! cast it out of the Bible? Canst thou take the penknife of Jehudi and cut it out of the Word of God? Wouldst thou be like the woman at the feet of Solomon, and have the child rent in halves, that thou mightest have thy half? Is it not here in Scripture? And is it not thy duty to bow before it, and meekly acknowledge what thou understandest not—to receive it as the truth even though thou couldst not understand its meaning? I will not attempt to prove the justice of God in having thus elected some and left others. It is not for me to vindicate my Master. He will speak for himself, and he does so: — "Nay, but, O man, who art thou that repliest against God? Shall the thing formed say to him that formed it, Why hast thou made me thus? Hath not the potter power over the clay of the same lump to make one vessel unto honour and another unto dishonour?" Who is he that shall say unto his father, "What hast thou begotten?" or unto his mother, "What hast thou brought forth?" "I am the Lord—I form the light and create darkness I, the Lord, do all these things." Who art thou that repliest against God? Tremble and kiss his rod; bow down and submit to his sceptre; impugn not his justice, and arraign not his acts before thy bar, O man!

But there are some who say, "It is hard for God to choose some and leave others." Now, I will ask you one question. Is there any of you here this morning who wishes to be holy, who wishes to be regenerate, to leave off sin and walk in holiness? "Yes, there is," says some one, "I do." Then God has elected you. But another says, "No; I don't want to be holy; I don't want to give up my lusts and my vices." Why should you grumble, then, that God has not elected you to it? For if you were elected you would not like it, according to your own confession. If God this morning had chosen you to holiness, you say you would not care for it. Do you not acknowledge that you prefer drunkenness to sobriety, dishonesty to honesty? You love this world's pleasures better than religion; then why should you grumble that God has not chosen you to religion? If you love religion, he has chosen you to it. If you desire it, he has chosen you to it. If you do not, what right have you to say that God ought to have given you what you do not wish for? Supposing I had in my hand something which you do not value, and I said I shall give it to such-and-such a person, you would have no right to grumble that I did not give to you. You could not be so foolish as to grumble that the other has got what you do not care about. According to your own confession, many of you do not want religion, do not want a new heart and a right spirit, do not want the forgiveness of sins, do not want sanctification; you do not want to be elected to these things: then why should you grumble? You count these things but as husks, and why should you complain of God who has given them to those whom he has chosen? If you believe them to be good and desire them, they are there for thee. God gives liberally to all those who desire; and first of all, he makes them desire, otherwise they never would. If you love these things, he has elected you to them, and you may have them; but if you do not, who are you that you should find fault with God, when it is your own desperate will that keeps you from loving these things—your own simple self that makes you hate them? Suppose a man in the street should say, "What a shame it is I cannot have a seat in the chapel to hear what this man has to say." And suppose he says, "I hate the preacher; I can't bear his doctrine; but still it's a shame I have not a seat." Would you expect a man to say so? No: you would at once say, "That man does not care for it. Why should he trouble himself about other people having what they value and he despises?" You do not like holiness, you do not like righteousness; if God has elected me to these things, has he hurt you by it? "Ah! but," say some, "I thought it meant that God elected some to heaven and some to hell." That is a very different matter from the gospel doctrine. He has elected men to holiness and to righteousness and through that to heaven. You must not say that he has elected them simply to heaven, and others only to hell. He has elected you to holiness, if you love holiness. If any of you love to be saved by Jesus Christ, Jesus Christ elected you to be saved. If any of you desire to have salvation, you are elected to have it, if you desire it sincerely and earnestly. But, if you don't desire it, why on earth should you be so preposterously foolish as to grumble because God gives that which you do not like to other people?

II. Thus I have tried to say something with regard to the truth of the doctrine of election. And now, briefly, let me say that election is ABSOLUTE: that is, it does not depend upon what we are. The text says, "God hath from the beginning chosen us unto salvation"; but our opponents say that God chooses people because they are good, that he chooses them on account of sundry works which they have done. Now, we ask in reply to this, what works are those on account of which God elects his people? Are they what we commonly call "works of law,"—works of obedience which the creature can render? If so, we reply to you—If men cannot be justified by the works of the law, it seems to us pretty clear that they cannot be elected by the works of the law: if they cannot be justified by their good deeds, they cannot be saved by them. Then the decree of election could not have been formed upon good works. "But," say others, "God elected them on the foresight of their faith." Now, God gives faith, therefore he could not have elected them on account of faith, which he foresaw. There shall be twenty beggars in the street, and I determine to give one of them a shilling; but will any one say that I determined to give that one a shilling, that I elected him to have the shilling, because I foresaw that he would have it? That would be talking nonsense. In like manner to say that God elected men because he foresaw they would have faith, which is salvation in the germ, would be too absurd for us to listen to for a moment. Faith is the gift of God. Every virtue comes from him. Therefore it cannot have caused him to elect men, because it is his gift. Election, we are sure, is absolute, and altogether apart from the virtues which the saints have afterwards. What though a saint should be as holy and devout as Paul; what though he should be as bold as Peter, or as loving as John, yet he would claim nothing from his Maker. I never knew a saint yet of any denomination, who thought that God saved him because he foresaw that he would have these virtues and merits. Now, my brethren, the best jewels that the saint ever wears, if they be jewels of his own fashioning, are not of the first water. There is something of earth mixed with them. The highest grace we ever possess has something of earthliness about it. We feel this when we are most refined, when we are most sanctified, and our language must always be—

"I the chief of sinners am;
Jesus died for me."

Our only hope, our only plea, still hangs on grace as exhibited in the person of Jesus Christ. And I am sure we must utterly reject and disregard all thought that our graces, which are gifts of our Lord, which are his right-hand planting, could have ever caused his love. And we ever must sing—

> *"What was there in us that could merit esteem*
> *Or give the Creator delight?*
> *'Twas even so Father we ever must sing,*
> *Because it seemed good in thy sight."*

"He will have mercy on whom he will have mercy": he saves because he will save. And if you ask me why he saves me, I can only say, because he would do it. Was there anything in me that should recommend me to God? No; I lay aside everything, I had nothing to recommend me. When God saved me I was the most abject, lost, and ruined of the race. I lay before him as an infant in my blood. Verily, I had no power to help myself. O how wretched did I feel and know myself to be! If you had something to recommend you to God, I never had. I will be content to be saved by grace, unalloyed, pure grace. I can boast of no merits. If you can do so, I cannot. I must sing—

> *"Free grace alone from the first to the last,*
> *Hath won my affection and held my soul fast."*

III. Then, thirdly, this election is ETERNAL. "God hath from the beginning chosen you unto eternal life." Can any man tell me when the beginning was? Years ago we thought the beginning of this world was when Adam came upon it; but we have discovered that thousands of years before that God was preparing chaotic matter to make it a fit abode for man, putting races of creatures upon it, who might die and leave behind the marks of his handiwork and marvellous skill, before he tried his hand on man. But that was not the beginning, for revelation points us to a period long ere this world was fashioned, to the days when the morning stars were begotten; when, like drops of dew, from the fingers of the morning, stars and constellations fell trickling from the hand of God; when, by his own lips, he launched forth ponderous orbs; when with his own hand he sent comets, like thunderbolts, wandering through the sky, to find one day their proper sphere. We go back to years gone by, when worlds were made and systems fashioned, but we have not even approached the beginning yet. Until we go to the time when all the universe slept in the mind of God as yet unborn, until we enter the eternity where God the Creator lived alone, everything sleeping within him, all creation resting in his mighty gigantic thought, we have not guessed the beginning. We may go back, back, back, ages upon ages. We may go back, if we might use such strange words, whole eternities, and yet never arrive at the beginning. Our wing might be tired, our imagination would die away; could it outstrip the lightnings flashing in majesty, power, and rapidity, it would soon weary itself ere it could get to the beginning. But God from the beginning chose his people; when the unnavigated ether was yet unfanned by the wing of a single angel, when space was shoreless, or else unborn when universal silence reigned, and not a voice or whisper shocked the solemnity of silence; when there was no being and no motion, no time, and nought but God himself, alone in his eternity; when without the song of an angel, without the attendance of even the cherubim, long ere the living creatures were born, or the wheels of the chariot of Jehovah were fashioned, even then, "in the beginning was the Word," and in the beginning God's people were one with the Word, and "in the beginning he chose them into eternal life." Our election then is eternal. I will not stop to prove it, I only just run over these thoughts for the benefit of young beginners, that they may understand what we mean by eternal, absolute election.

IV. And, next, the election is PERSONAL. Here again, our opponents have tried to overthrow election by telling us that it is an election of nations, and not of people. But here the Apostle says, "God hath from the beginning chosen you." It is the most miserable shift on earth to make out that God hath not chosen persons but nations, because the very same objection that lies against the choice of persons, lies against the choice of a nation. If it were not just to choose a person, it would be far more unjust to choose a nation, since nations are but the union of multitudes of persons, and to choose a nation seems to be a more gigantic crime—if election be a crime—than to choose one person. Surely to choose ten thousand would be reckoned to be worse than choosing one; to distinguish a whole nation from the rest of mankind, does seem to be a greater extravaganza in the acts of divine sovereignty than the election of one poor mortal and leaving out another. But what are nations but men? What are whole peoples but combinations of different units? A nation is made up of that individual, and that, and that. And if you tell me that God chose the Jews, I say then, he chose that Jew, and that Jew, and that Jew. And if you say he chooses Britain, then I say he chooses that British man, and that British man, and that British man. So that is the same thing after all. Election then is personal: it must be so. Every one who reads this text, and others like it, will see that Scripture continually speaks of God's people one by one and speaks of them as having been the special subjects of election.

"Sons we are through God's election,
Who in Jesus Christ believe;
By eternal destination
Sovereign grace we here receive."

We know it is personal election.

V. The other thought is—for my time flies too swiftly to enable me to dwell at length upon these points— that election produces GOOD RESULTS. "He hath from the beginning chosen you unto sanctification of the spirit, and belief of the truth." How many men mistake the doctrine of election altogether! and how my soul burns and boils at the recollection of the terrible evils that have accrued from the spoiling and the wresting of that glorious portion of God's glorious truth! How many are there who have said to themselves, "I am elect," and have sat down in sloth, and worse than that! They have said, "I am the elect of God," and with both hands they have done wickedness. They have swiftly run to every unclean thing, because they have said, "I am the chosen child of God, irrespective of my works, therefore I may live as I list, and do what I like." Oh, beloved! let me solemnly warn every one of you not to carry the truth too far; or, rather not to turn the truth into error, for we cannot carry it too far. We may overstep the truth; we can make that which was meant to be sweet for our comfort, a terrible mixture for our destruction. I tell you there have been thousands of men who have been ruined by misunderstanding election; who have said, "God has elected me to heaven, and to eternal life"; but they have forgotten that it is written, God has elected them "through sanctification of the Spirit and belief of the truth." This is God's election—election to sanctification and to faith. God chooses his people to be holy, and to be believers. How many of you here then are believers? How many of my congregation can put their hands upon their hearts and say, "I trust in God that I am sanctified"? Is there one of you who says, "I am elect"?—I remind that you swore last week. One of you says, "I trust I am elect"—but I jog your memory about some vicious act that you committed during the last six days. Another of you says, "I am elect"—but I would look you in the face and say, "Elect! thou art a most cursed hypocrite! and that is all thou art." Others would say, "I am elect"—but I would remind them that they neglect the mercy-seat and do not pray. Oh, beloved! never think you are elect unless you are holy. You may come to Christ as a sinner, but you may not come to Christ as an elect person until you can see your holiness. Do not misconstrue what I say—do not say "I am elect," and yet think you can be living in sin. That is impossible. The elect of God are holy. They are not pure, they are not perfect, they are not spotless; but, taking their life as a whole, they are holy persons. They are marked, and distinct from others: and no man has a right to conclude himself elect except in his holiness. He may be elect, and yet lying in darkness, but he has no right to believe it; no one can see it, there is no evidence of it. The man may live one day, but he is dead at present. If you are walking in the fear of God, trying to please him, and to obey his commandments, doubt not that your name has been written in the Lamb's book of life from before the foundation of the world.

And, lest this should be too high for you, note the other mark of election, which is faith, "belief of the truth." Whoever believes God's truth, and believes on Jesus Christ, is elect. I frequently meet with poor souls, who are fretting and worrying themselves about this thought — "How, if I should not be elect!" "Oh, sir," they say, "I know I put my trust in Jesus; I know I believe in his name and trust in his blood; but how if I should not be elect?" Poor dear creature! you do not know much about the gospel, or you would never talk so, for he that believes is elect. Those who are elect, are elect unto sanctification and unto faith; and if you have faith you are one of God's elect; you may know it and ought to know it, for it is an absolute certainty. If you, as a sinner, look to Jesus Christ this morning, and say—

> *"Nothing in my hands I bring,*
> *Simply to thy cross I cling,"*

you are elect. I am not afraid of election frightening poor saints or sinners. There are many divines who tell the enquirer "election has nothing to do with you." That is very bad, because the poor soul is not to be silenced like that. If you could silence him so, it might be well, but he will think of it, he can't help it. Say to him then, if you believe on the Lord Jesus Christ you are elect. If you will cast yourself on Jesus, you are elect. I tell you—the chief of sinners—this morning, I tell you in his name, if you will come to God without any works of your own, cast yourself on the blood and righteousness of Jesus Christ; if you will come now and trust in him, you are elect—you were loved of God from before the foundation of the world, for you could not do that unless God had given you the power, and had chosen you to do it. Now you are safe and secure if you do but come and cast yourself on Jesus Christ, and wish to be saved and to be loved by him. But think not that any man will be saved without faith and without holiness. Do not conceive, my hearers, that some decree, passed in the dark ages of eternity, will save your souls, unless you believe in Christ. Do not sit down and fancy that you are to be saved without faith and holiness. That is a most abominable and accursed heresy, and has ruined thousands. Lay not election as a pillow for you to sleep on, or you may be ruined.

God forbid that I should be sewing pillows under armholes that you may rest comfortably in your sins. Sinner! there is nothing in the Bible to palliate your sins. But if thou art condemned O man! if thou art lost O woman! thou wilt not find in this Bible one drop to cool thy tongue, or one doctrine to palliate thy guilt; your damnation will be entirely your own fault, and your sin will richly merit it, because ye believe not ye are condemned. "Ye believe not because ye are not of my sheep." "Ye wilt not come to me that ye might have life." Do not fancy that election excuses sin—do not dream of it—do not rock yourself in sweet complacency in the thought of your irresponsibility. You are responsible. We must give you both things. We must have divine sovereignty, and we must have man's responsibility. We must have election, but we must ply your hearts, we must send God's truth at you; we must speak to you, and remind you of this, that while it is written, "In me is thy help"; yet it is also written, "O Israel, thou hast destroyed thyself."

VI. Now, lastly, what are the true and legitimate tendencies of right conceptions concerning the doctrine of election. First, I will tell you what the doctrine of election will make saints do under the blessing of God;

and, secondly what it will do for sinners if God blesses it to them.

First, I think election, to a saint, is one of the most stripping doctrines in all the world— to take away all trust in the flesh, or all reliance upon anything except Jesus Christ. How often do we wrap ourselves up in our own righteousness, and array ourselves with the false pearls and gems of our own works and doings. We begin to say "Now I shall be saved, because I have this and that evidence." Instead of that, it is naked faith that saves; that faith and that alone unites to the Lamb, irrespective of works, although it is productive of them. How often do we lean on some work, other than that of our own Beloved, and trust in some might, other than that which comes from on high. Now if we would have this might taken from us, we must consider election. Pause my soul, and consider this. God loved thee before thou hadst a being. He loved thee when thou wast dead in trespasses and sins, and sent his Son to die for thee. He purchased thee with his precious blood ere thou couldst lisp his name. Canst thou then be proud?

I know nothing, nothing again, that is more humbling for us than this doctrine of election. I have sometimes fallen prostrate before it, when endeavouring to understand it. I have stretched my wings, and, eagle-like, I have soared towards the sun. Steady has been my eye, and true my wing, for a season; but, when I came near it, and the one thought possessed me, — "God hath from the beginning chosen you unto salvation," I was lost in its lustre, I was staggered with the mighty thought; and from the dizzy elevation down came my soul, prostrate and broken, saying, "Lord, I am nothing, I am less than nothing. Why me? Why me?"

Friends, if you want to be humbled, study election, for it will make you humble under the influence of God's Spirit. He who is proud of his election is not elect; and he who is humbled under a sense of it may believe that he is. He has every reason to believe that he is, for it is one of the most blessed effects of election that it helps us to humble ourselves before God.

Once again. Election in the Christian should make him very fearless and very bold. No man will be so bold as he who believes that he is elect of God. What cares he for man if he is chosen of his Maker? What will he care for the pitiful chirpings of some tiny sparrows when he knoweth that he is an eagle of a royal race? Will he care when the beggar pointeth at him, when the blood royal of heaven runs in his veins? Will he fear if all the world stand against him? If earth be all in arms abroad, he dwells in perfect peace, for he is in the secret place of the tabernacle of the Most High, in the great pavillion of the Almighty. "I am God's," says he, "I am distinct from other men. They are of an inferior race. Am not I noble? Am not I one of the aristocrats of heaven? Is not my name written in God's book?" Does he care for the world? Nay: like the lion that careth not for the barking of the dog, he smileth at all his enemies; and when they come too near him, he moveth himself and dasheth them to pieces. What careth he for them? He walks about them like a colossus; while little men walk under him and understand him not. His brow is made of iron, his heart is of flint—what doth he care for man? Nay; if one universal hiss came up from the wide world, he would smile at it, for he would say,—

"He that hath made his refuge God,
Shall find a most secure abode."

"I am one of his elect. I am chosen of God and precious; and though the world cast me out, I fear not." Ah! ye time-serving professors, some of you can bend like the willows. There are few oaken-Christians now-a-days, that can stand the storm; and I will tell you the reason. It is because you do not believe yourselves to be elect. The man who knows he is elect will be too proud to sin; he will not humble himself to commit the acts of common people. The believer in this truth will say, "I compromise my principles? I change my doctrines? I lay aside my views? I hide what I believe to be true? No! since I know I am one of God's elect, in the very teeth of all men I shall speak God's truth, whatever man may say." Nothing makes a man so truly bold as to feel that he is God's elect. He shall not quiver, he shall not shake, who knows that God has chosen him.

Moreover, election will make us holy. Nothing under the gracious influence of the Holy Spirit can make a Christian more holy than the thought that he is chosen. "Shall I sin," he says, "after God hath chosen me? Shall I transgress after such love? Shall I go astray after so much lovingkindness and tender mercy? Nay, my God; since thou hast chosen me, I will love thee; I will live to thee—

'Since thou, the everlasting God,
My Father art become;'

I will give myself to thee to be thine for ever, by election and by redemption, casting myself on thee, and solemnly consecrating myself to thy service."

And now, lastly, to the ungodly. What says election to you? First, ye ungodly ones, I will excuse you for a moment. There are many of you who do not like election, and I cannot blame you for it, for I have heard those preach election, who have sat down, and said, "I have not one word to say to the sinner." Now, I say you ought to dislike such preaching as that, and I do not blame you for it. But, I say, take courage, take hope, O thou sinner, that there is election. So far from dispiriting and discouraging thee, it is a very hopeful and joyous thing that there is an election. What if I told thee perhaps none can be saved, none are ordained to eternal life; wouldst thou not tremble and fold thy hands in hopelessness, and say, "Then how can I be saved, since none are elect?" But, I say, there is a multitude elect, beyond all counting—a host that no mortal can number. Therefore, take heart, thou poor sinner! Cast away thy despondency—mayest thou not be elect as well as any other? for there is a host innumerable chosen. There is joy and comfort for thee! Then, not only take heart, but go and try the Master. Remember, if you were not elect, you would lose nothing by it. What did the four Syrians say? "Let us fall unto the host of the Syrians, for if we stay here we must die, and if we go to them we can but die." O sinner! come to the throne of electing mercy, Thou mayest die where thou art. Go to God; and, even supposing he should spurn thee, suppose his uplifted hand should drive thee away—a thing impossible—yet thou wilt not lose anything; thou wilt not be more damned for that. Besides, supposing thou be damned, thou wouldst have the satisfaction at least of being able to lift up thine eyes in hell and say, "God, I asked mercy of thee and thou wouldst not grant it; I sought it, but thou didst refuse it." That thou never shalt say, O sinner! If thou goest to him, and askest him, thou shalt receive; for he ne'er has spurned one yet! Is not that hope for you? What though there is an allotted number, yet it is true that all who seek belong to that number. Go thou and seek; and if thou shouldst be the first one to go to hell, tell the devils that thou didst perish thus—tell the demons that thou art a castaway, after having come as a guilty sinner to Jesus. I tell thee it would disgrace the Eternal—with reverence to his name—and he would not allow such a thing. He is jealous of his honour, and he could not allow a sinner to say that.

But ah, poor soul! not only think thus, that thou canst not lose anything by coming; there is yet one more thought— dost thou love the thought of election this morning? Art thou willing to admit its justice? Dost thou say, "I feel that I am lost; I deserve it; and that if my brother is saved I cannot murmur. If God destroy me, I deserve it, but if he saves the person sitting beside me, he has a right to do what he will with his own, and I have lost nothing by it." Can you say that honestly from your heart? If so, then the doctrine of election has had its right effect on your spirit, and you are not far from the kingdom of heaven. You are brought where you ought to be, where the Spirit wants you to be; and being so this morning, depart in peace; God has forgiven your sins. You would not feel that if you were not pardoned; you would not feel that if the Spirit of God were not working in you. Rejoice, then, in this. Let your hope rest on the cross of Christ. Think not on election but on Christ Jesus. Rest on Jesus—Jesus first, midst, and without end.

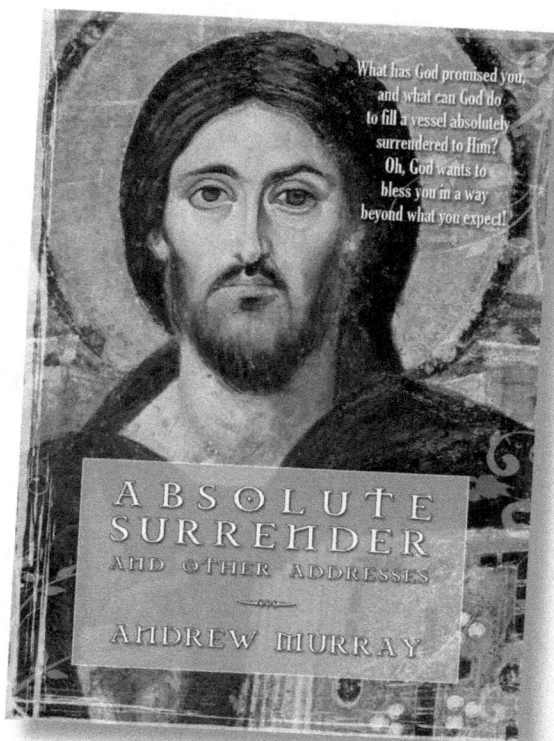

ABSOLUTE SURRENDER
by Andrew Murray

I want to use these words: "My lord, O king, according to thy saying, I am thine, and all that I have," as the words of absolute surrender with which every child of God ought to yield himself to his Father. We have heard it before, but we need to hear it very definitely — the condition of God's blessing is absolute surrender of all into His hands. Praise God! If our hearts are willing for that, there is no end to what God will do for us, and to the blessing God will bestow.

What has God promised you, and what can God do to fill a vessel absolutely surrendered to Him? Oh, God wants to bless you in a way beyond what you expect!

Perfect Bound, BW, 6x9 — (ISBN# 1-60039-150-8) 116 Pages, $7.00